Dear God,

I WATCHED MY MUM TODAY,
SHE REALLY LOVES TO COOK.
I THOUGHT THAT SHE INVENTED IT,
BUT SHE GETS IT FROM A BOOK!

Dear God Kids

OUR family

ROGER KNIGHTS
PICTURES BY Annie

Purnell

Dear God,

Do you make bicycles?
They're such a lot of fun.
And if you do, would you come here
to try and make me one?

Dear God,

I HAVE A SECRET PLACE,
WHERE I GO WITH MY TEDDY,
BUT YOU DON'T NEED TO FIND OUT WHERE,
I'M SURE YOU KNOW ALREADY.

Dear God,

THEY SAY I LOOK LIKE DAD,
BUT I THINK THAT IS WEIRD
BECAUSE I AM A LITTLE GIRL
AND HE HAS GOT A BEARD.

Dear God,

You fix all kinds of things.
Does that include TVs?
Ours broke down just yesterday—
Could you mend it, please?

Dear God,

I wish that I was tall,
as tall as my big brother.
But when I grow an inch or two,
he always grows another.

Dear God,

WHEN I'M TUCKED UP AT NIGHT,
SO SNUGLY IN MY BED,
I KNOW THAT YOU'VE BEEN LISTENING TO
THE LITTLE PRAYERS I'VE SAID.

Dear God,

I need your help today,
as I am rather late.
Would you just look and let me know
if my ribbon's straight?

Dear God,

although I'm only very small
it's lucky that I know
that if I eat my breakfast
my mother says I'll grow.

Dear God,

DO YOU HAVE BROTHERS, TOO?
I HOPE YOU DO, LIKE ME.
THEN YOU MUST KNOW ALL ABOUT
THE FUN THAT THEY CAN BE.

Dear God,

I'm on my holidays
with sun and sea and sand.
I'd like to go out paddling,
so will you hold my hand?

Dear God,

I'M ON MY HOLIDAYS
WITH SUN AND SEA AND SAND.
I'D LIKE TO GO OUT PADDLING,
SO WILL YOU HOLD MY HAND?

Dear God,

If I'm a naughty boy,
I know you always see.
But if my daddy doesn't,
would you tell on me?

Dear God,

I wonder if you're tired
with all the things you do?
If you would only show me how,
could I make something too?

Dear God,

If ONLY I was TaLL,
I'D GET To see MUCH MORE,
BUT BEING SMALL, I HaVE To GUESS
WHO'S KNOCKING aT THE DOOR.

Dear God,

I'D LiKE To THaNK YoU
foR GIViNG Me THiS DaY.
IT'S fulL of Peace aND QUIeT Because
MY BROTHeR iS awaY.

Dear God,

Tonight we put our presents around the Christmas tree. Tomorrow is **YOUR** birthday, but it's a special day for me!

Dear God,

THANK YOU FOR THE SEASONS,
THE WIND, THE RAIN, AND SUN.
IF WE DIDN'T HAVE A WINTER
SPRING WOULDN'T BE SUCH FUN.

This book was devised and produced by
Multimedia Publications (UK) Ltd.

First published 1984 by
Purnell Books, Paulton, Bristol BS18 5LQ.
A member of the BPCC group of companies.
By arrangement with Multimedia Publications (UK) Ltd.

Illustrations copyright © 1984 INTERCONTINENTAL GREETINGS LTD
Illustrations by Anne Fitzgerald
Text copyright © 1984 Roger Knights
This edition copyright © 1984 Multimedia Publications (UK) Ltd
All rights reserved.

ISBN 0 361 06656 2

Originated by D.S. Colour International Ltd.
Printed in Italy by New Interlitho.